Healthy Cooking for Your Dog:

Wholesome Recipes for a Long, Happy Life

Library of Congress Cataloging-in-Publication Data
Title: Healthy Cooking for Your Dog: Wholesome Recipes for a Long, Happy Life
LCCN: 2025901312

BISAC Subject Categories:
COO020000 – Cooking / Pet Food
PET004000 – Pets / Dogs / General
HEA019000 – Health & Fitness / Nutrition

Hardcover ISBNs:
979-8-9922548-2-2

eBook ISBNs:
979-8-9922548-1-5

Disclaimer:

The recipes in this book have been reviewed by a veterinarian to ensure they are generally safe and nutritious for dogs. However, each dog has unique dietary needs, allergies, and sensitivities. Your use of the information in this book is at your own risk and should be used in conjunction with the guidance and care of your veterinarian. Do not rely upon any information to replace consultation or advice provided by your veterinarian. Consult with your veterinarian before introducing new foods into your dog's diet, particularly if your dog has existing health conditions or dietary restrictions. None of the recipes in this book are to be used for your dogs daily nutritional needs; responsible feeding practices are strongly encouraged. The author and publisher disclaim liability for any negative or other medical outcomes that may occur as a result of your acting on or not acting on the recipes or anything set forth in this book, including without limitation any adverse reactions or health issues that may occur to your dog as a result of following or not following the recipes. The recipes are not to be used for consumption by any animals other than dogs.

Veterinarian Consultant by Dr. Deborah Patterson, DVM, MS
Design by Jennifer Okada
Copy Edited by Erin Harnum
First Edition
Printed in the United States and/or other locations

LEW DOG GIVES
Love & Hope for Animals

Lewie's Legacy

Lew Dog Gives is a nonprofit devoted to creating a kinder world where all animals are safe, loved, and valued.

Inspired by Lewie—our soul-dog and guiding light—we turn love into action, raising funds to support animals in need and the people who care for them. From sanctuaries to rescues, emergency aid to everyday comfort, every donation brings nourishment, healing, shelter, and hope.

This cookbook is one way we give back—with every recipe, we honor the bond between us and the animals who change our lives.

Learn more at LewDogGives.org

To Lewie, my soul dog, who showed me
how to love unconditionally. Even in the
afterlife, he continues to show me the
importance of spreading love to others.

Contents

Introduction

I've always loved animals; I can remember as a small child loving anything that had wings or legs, especially dogs. That love has grown over a lifetime and changed my life when I met my soul-dog Lewie.

Lewie taught me what it means to feel unconditional love. Through that love, I began to recognize that I was afforded a gift that would change my life for the better.

That's where this book begins. This book is for all of the humans who hold their dogs and all animals closest to their heart. It's meant to elevate your dog's health so you can spend more valuable time loving one another.

I also created this book to give back to animals in need. All net proceeds will go towards communities who care for animals of all kinds. Animals who've been abandoned or mistreated and need a loving place in this world. By buying and supporting this book you are helping animals who deserve a second chance at life.

We are guardians of these precious souls; not owners. There doesn't seem to be enough time to experience all of our animals joy, funny antics, and love. Although I've spent a lifetime learning about food for myself and overall health, I'm seeing how food and good living can heal both humans and dogs.

In fact, the recipe for longevity happens to be the same for dogs and humans. Good nutrition, getting daily exercise, and sniffing flowers along the way leads to greater health and happiness. Add to that a low stress environment, being surrounded by family and friends, and most importantly lots of love provides a greater and enriching quality of life.

What I would give to have more years with Lewie. I have so many fond memories of him being right by my side in the kitchen. He was always willing to be my taster and never complained about any food he ate... except peas. And that's ok with me.

This is my contribution to all animals and the world. My universal mission is to love, respect and guard these beautiful souls.

I am thankful you are joining me on this journey to spread love. Together we can bring more kindness, care, and joy to the world.

Safe and Happy Feeding Tips for Your Pup

Every dog is unique. It's always wise to check with your veterinarian before adding new foods to their diet—especially if your pup has specific health needs. Let's keep those tails wagging safely!

- Avoid harmful seasonings and additives, such as salt, spices, and butter.

- Adjust portion sizes based on your dog's size and dietary needs.

- Modify recipes for dogs with specific allergies or sensitivities, or consult your veterinarian.

- Always serve food at an appropriate temperature; ensure no hot spots before feeding.

Important Reminder

Consult your veterinarian before introducing new foods, especially if your dog has health conditions.

The recipes in this book are intended for both dogs and humans, but always practice responsible feeding and consult your veterinarian for dietary changes.

Many homemade diets can be nutritionally deficient. Please consult your veterinarian for the appropriate nutrients for a balanced diet. The Association of American Feed Control Officials (AAFCO) provides recommendations for dog food nutrients including calcium, vitamins A and E, zinc, copper, and potassium.

What's the Right Food Portion for My Dog?

Determining the right amount of food for your dog depends on various factors, including age, size, weight, and health. Puppies, pregnant dogs, adults, and seniors all have unique dietary needs. If you're unsure about portion sizes or feeding frequency, check with your veterinarian for guidance. Additionally, you can find food calculators online—just make sure to choose one that's designed for fresh, homemade meals.

Pawsitively Safe and Unsuitable: A Guide to Dog-Friendly Foods and Herbs

Always introduce new herbs and foods slowly while keeping an eye on your dog for any signs of discomfort or allergic reactions. Check the safe and unsafe herbs and foods below to help keep your pup healthy. This is not an exhaustive list, but it's a great place to start. When in doubt, check with your veterinarian to make sure the herbs and foods are safe and suitable for your furry friend.

Safe Herbs

Many herbs provide benefits for your dog's health and can help elevate a nutritious meal. Use these herbs in moderation. Some dogs may have allergies or sensitivities to certain herbs, so monitor your dog for any adverse reactions.

Basil: Antioxidant-rich with anti-inflammatory benefits.

Chamomile: Calming; helps with anxiety and sleep.

Cilantro: Supports detoxification with antioxidants.

Cinnamon: Regulates blood sugar and provides antioxidants (use sparingly).

Dill: Aids digestion and freshens breath.

Echinacea: Boosts immunity and overall health.

Ginger: Supports digestion, reduces nausea, and fights inflammation.

Lemon Balm: Promotes relaxation and eases anxiety.

Marshmallow Root: Soothes digestion and reduces inflammation.

Mint: Calms the stomach and freshens breath.

Oregano: Antimicrobial and immune-boosting; use oregano oil sparingly.

Parsley: Aids digestion and freshens breath.

Peppermint: Soothes digestion and freshens breath.

Rosemary: Antioxidant-rich, aids digestion, and acts as a preservative.

Sage: Supports oral health, immunity, and digestion when used in moderation.

Thyme: Antioxidant and antiseptic properties.

Turmeric: Powerful anti-inflammatory; supports joints, immunity, and digestion.

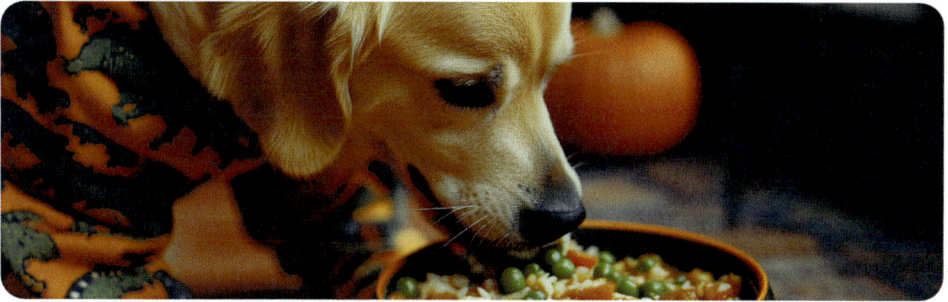

Safe Foods

Numerous foods are nutritious and provide health benefits for dogs. Be sure to chop the foods into bite-sized pieces to aid digestion and prevent choking hazards. Here's a list of tasty ingredients to whip up delicious meals and snacks:

Barley: Cooked barley adds fiber and nutrients.

Black Beans: Cooked, unseasoned black beans provide protein and fiber (in moderation).

Carob: A dog-safe alternative to chocolate; avoid added sugars or artificial sweeteners.

Chia Seeds: Rich in omega-3s and fiber; serve a small amount soaked or ground.

Coconut: Coconut meat, oil, and flour provide healthy fats and can also have potential benefits for the skin and coat; introduce gradually.

Coconut Water: Natural, unsweetened coconut water is a hydrating treat and electrolyte-rich beverage in moderation.

Cottage Cheese: A protein and calcium-rich snack; choose unsweetened, low-fat varieties.

Cranberries: Raw or cooked cranberries are antioxidant-rich, but avoid sweetened versions.

Edamame: Steamed or boiled edamame is a protein-rich treat. Remove the beans from the pods before offering them.

Eggs: Cooked eggs offer high-quality protein.

Fish: Cooked fish (salmon, mackerel, sardines, and tuna in moderation) provides omega-3s which are beneficial for your dog's skin, coat, and overall health; ensure no bones.

Fruits: Safe options include apples, bananas, bell peppers, blueberries, cucumbers, kiwi, and melons—remove seeds, pits, and rinds. Mango, pears, pomegranate (small amounts deseeded), and oranges (peeled, seedless) are nutritious but should be fed in moderation due to their sugar content. Oranges may not suit all dogs due to their acidity.

Lentils: Cooked lentils offer fiber and plant-based protein.

Meats: Lean, cooked, boneless, skinless meats (chicken, turkey, beef, pork) are great protein sources. Avoid seasoning or sauces that are harmful to dogs.

Oatmeal: Plain, cooked oatmeal is a good fiber source.

Peanut Butter: Natural, unsalted peanut butter is a tasty treat; avoid xylitol.

Popcorn: Plain, air-popped popcorn is a low-calorie snack.

Pumpkin: Plain canned (not pumpkin pie filling) or cooked pumpkin is a good source of fiber and aids digestion.

Quinoa: Cooked quinoa provides protein, fiber, and essential minerals.

Rice: Cooked brown or white rice is easy to digest and provides extra fiber.

Seaweed: Plain nori or dulse offers vitamins and minerals. Ensure it is free from any seasonings or additives.

Vegetables: Dogs can benefit from a variety of vegetables, including artichokes, beets, broccoli, brussels sprouts (cooked), carrots, cauliflower, celery, green beans, peas, parsnips, pumpkin (cooked), radishes, sweet potatoes (cooked), and zucchini. Cooking certain vegetables aids digestion and reduces choking risks.

Leafy Greens: Nutrient-rich greens like arugula, collard greens, kale, lettuce, and spinach provide vitamins and minerals. Chop into bite-sized pieces for easier digestion.

Tomatoes (Botanically a fruit, culinarily a vegetable): Ripe tomatoes are safe in small amounts, providing vitamins and antioxidants. However, avoid leaves, stems, and unripe fruit, as they can be toxic.

Wheat Germ and Wheatgrass: Good sources of vitamins and minerals, and antioxidants; introduce gradually.

Yogurt: Plain, unsweetened yogurt or Greek yogurt is probiotic-rich.

Unsafe Foods and Herbs

Several foods are deemed unsafe or toxic for dogs; it's crucial to keep these out of your pup's diet. Feeding them these foods can lead to a range of health problems, from gastrointestinal distress to organ damage—and in some cases, they can even be life-threatening. Although this isn't a complete list, here are some examples:

Alcohol and Alcohol-Based Extracts: Even small amounts of alcohol (including vanilla and almond extracts) can cause poisoning which can lead to vomiting, disorientation, breathing issues, abnormal blood acidity, coma, or death.

Artificial Flavorings and Additives: Preservatives, sweeteners, and flavor enhancers such as certain sweeteners or food colorings may cause digestive issues or allergic reactions.

Avocado: The flesh is safe in small amounts, but the pit, skin, and leaves contain persin, which can be toxic.

Bones and Fat Trimmings: Bones can splinter, causing choking, blockages or internal injuries. Fatty scraps can lead to pancreatitis. Even raw bones, often considered safer, can carry harmful bacteria like Salmonella.

Caffeine: Found in coffee, tea, energy drinks, soda, and some medications. It can cause rapid breathing, increased heart rate, tremors, seizures, and, in severe cases, be fatal.

Chives, Onions and Garlic: Allium family plants can damage red blood cells, leading to anemia. Symptoms include weakness, pale gums, elevated heart rate, and in severe cases can cause your dog to collapse.

Chocolate: Contains theobromine and caffeine, both toxic to dogs. Dark chocolate is the most dangerous. Consumption can cause vomiting, diarrhea, increased heart rate, seizures, or death. If your dog ingests chocolate, contact your veterinarian immediately.

Dairy Products: Many dogs are lactose intolerant. Small amounts of plain, low-fat dairy may be tolerated, but excess can cause digestive upset.

Deli Meats: High in sodium, additives, and allergens. May cause dehydration, allergies, and digestive upset.

High-Fat Foods: Fatty meats, butter, and fried foods increase the risk of pancreatitis, causing vomiting, appetite loss, and abdominal pain.

Fruits with Seeds/Pits: Apples, pears, and peaches are safe if seeds and pits are removed. However, persimmons, peaches, plums, apricots, and cherries contain cyanide, which is toxic, and pose choking or blockage risks. Always remove seeds, pits, leaves, and stems before feeding these fruits.

Grapes and Raisins: Even small amounts can be toxic and may cause kidney failure. Symptoms include vomiting, diarrhea, lethargy, and loss of appetite. Seek immediate veterinary care if ingested.

Moldy or Spoiled Food: Can contain toxins or harmful bacteria like Salmonella. Keep trash and compost out of reach.

Mushrooms: Certain varieties of mushrooms can be toxic to dogs. Eating wild mushrooms can cause gastrointestinal upset, liver damage, and in some cases, organ failure.

Nutmeg: Nutmeg is toxic to dogs and can cause symptoms like stomach pain, hallucinations, disorientation, increased heart rate, and seizures.

Nuts: Almonds, macadamia nuts, walnuts, and pecans can cause weakness, tremors, vomiting, overheating, and digestive issues. They also pose a choking hazard, and some nuts contain toxins harmful to dogs.

Raw Seafood: Raw seafood, such as raw fish or shellfish, can contain harmful parasites and bacteria that can cause gastrointestinal issues in dogs. Additionally, certain fish such as salmon and trout can contain a parasite called Neorickettsia helminthoeca, which can lead to a potentially fatal condition known as salmon poisoning disease.

Raw or Undercooked Meat and Eggs: Can contain parasites or bacteria (e.g., Salmonella, E. coli) that cause food poisoning. Always cook thoroughly.

Rhubarb: The leaves contain toxic oxalates that can harm kidneys. Although rhubarb stalks are safe in small amounts, the leaves should always be avoided due to their toxicity.

Salt: Excess salt from snacks and processed foods can cause poisoning, leading to dehydration, tremors, seizures, and, in severe cases, death.

Sweeteners and Xylitol: Artificial sweeteners like aspartame (Amino-Sweet), sucralose, saccharin, and stevia can cause digestive upset or poisoning. Xylitol, found in sugar-free gum, candy, and some peanut butter, is highly toxic, triggering a rapid insulin release that leads to life-threatening hypoglycemia. Symptoms include vomiting, loss of coordination, seizures, and liver failure. Xylitol ingestion is an emergency—seek immediate veterinary care.

Tuna (Canned in Oil or Seasoned): Plain, cooked tuna is fine, but canned versions often contain harmful additives.

Unripe Green Tomatoes and Leaves: Green tomatoes and their leaves contain solanine, which is toxic and can cause digestive upset, lethargy, or more severe reactions.

Yeast Dough: Raw dough expands in the stomach, causing bloating or obstruction. Fermentation produces alcohol, leading to poisoning. Seek immediate veterinary care if ingested.

The Basics: Tasty Meals for Every Tail-Wagger

These simple recipes make it easy to stock up and keep your pup's meals exciting all week long. They're also a great base for many of the tasty dishes in this book. Meal prep isn't just for humans—having ready-to-go food speeds up meal time, which is a lifesaver when your dog's giving you that "I'm starving" look! My dog Lewie was as food-motivated as I am, and honestly, both of us would start drooling just thinking about the next meal. Because, let's face it, good food is worth a little excitement.

Easy Gravy

Who doesn't like gravy? Mmmmmm. What more can a dog ask for.

Ingredients

1 tablespoon coconut oil or beef tallow

1 tablespoon flour (you can use whole wheat or gluten-free flour as alternatives)

1 cup low-sodium chicken or beef broth

Directions

In a small saucepan, heat the coconut oil or beef tallow over medium heat.

Add the flour to the saucepan and whisk continuously for about 1-2 minutes, until the flour mixture is lightly toasted and golden in color.

Slowly pour the chicken or beef broth into the saucepan, whisking constantly to prevent lumps from forming.

Continue to whisk the mixture over medium heat until it thickens and reaches a gravy-like consistency. This usually takes about 5 minutes.

Remove the saucepan from the heat and let the gravy cool down before serving it over delicious meals for your dog.

Bone Broth Bliss: A Nutritious Boost for Your Pup

Homemade bone broth is more than just delicious—it's a nutritious addition to your dog's diet. Packed with collagen and minerals, it helps support joint health, digestion, and hydration. Pour it over meals for extra flavor or serve it warm on its own for a cozy treat that'll have tails wagging.

Bow WOW Bone Broth

Your pup's nose will be working overtime when this broth is simmering. You might want to use it too—think soups or even a healthy warm cup of nutrients — because homemade broth makes the taste buds say yes! Plus, it's a nutritious addition to your dog's diet providing minerals, collagen, and a flavorful addition to meals. Just watch out—they may not leave the kitchen until you serve it up!

Ingredients

2-3 pounds of raw bones (such as chicken, turkey, beef, or pork bones)

Water (enough to cover the bones in the pot)

2 tablespoons apple cider vinegar

2 carrots washed and halved

2 celery sticks washed and halved

1 bunch parsley

Small pinch of sea salt

Directions

Roast the raw bones on a baking sheet at 400°F (200°C) for 30 minutes. Roasting the bones enhances the flavor of the broth.

Transfer roasted bones to a large pot, add water (enough to cover the bones), and the apple cider vinegar (to help extract nutrients from the bones).

Add the carrots, celery, and parsley.

Bring the pot to a boil, then reduce the heat to low and let it simmer for at least 4-6 hours. The longer the simmer, the more nutrients will be extracted from the bones.

Periodically skim off any foam or impurities that rise to the surface during simmering.

After simmering, remove the pot from the heat, add the salt while it's still warm and let the broth cool.

Strain the broth to remove the bones and vegetables, ensuring you have a clear liquid.

Allow the bone broth to cool completely before serving or storing it.

Store the bone broth in the refrigerator for up to 4-5 days, or freeze it in smaller portions for later use. A layer of fat may solidify on top. The fat has lots of nutrients and can be used to cook other meals.

Juicy Shredded Chicken

Get ready for the dish that'll have your dog drooling the second they catch a whiff. My dog Lewie and I both love this Juicy Shredded Chicken and often had it on hand to add to any dish—his and mine!

Ingredients

4 Boneless, skinless chicken breasts or thighs

Salt

Broth (low-sodium chicken) or water

Directions

Place chicken in a medium metal or glass bowl and lightly coat with salt. Cover and refrigerate for 30 minutes.

Remove the chicken from the refrigerator, discard any liquid from the bowl.

Transfer the chicken to a large pot. Pour broth or water over the meat so that it is covered.

Turn the heat to medium-high until it comes to a boil. Once it starts to boil, immediately reduce the heat to a simmer. Place a lid over the pot and let it simmer for about 10 minutes or until cooked. If using a thermometer, insert it into the thickest part of the breast and rest the probe in the center. The chicken will be ready at 165°F (74°C).

Once cooked, transfer to a cutting board and let rest for 10 minutes. Start shredding with a fork or your fingers.

Serve the cooked chicken to your dog as a stand-alone treat or mix it with other meals.

Secrets to Tender Chicken

Start with a cold pot and broth and then allow the chicken to rise in temperature. Keep the liquid at a simmer. Boiling will cause the chicken to be rubbery.

Roasted Turkey

Here's a meal base that'll have your pup doing a happy dance! Dice up this Roasted Turkey after cooking and stash the extras in the fridge (if your dog doesn't claim it all first). Just remember to cook thoroughly, remove skin, bones, and extra fat, and maybe sneak a little to make a turkey sandwich for yourself.

Ingredients

1 pound boneless turkey breast or turkey thigh, skin removed

1 tablespoon olive oil

Directions

Preheat your oven to 350°F (175°C).

Place the boneless turkey breast or turkey thigh in a baking dish.

Drizzle the olive oil over the turkey and rub it into the meat to coat it evenly.

Cover the baking dish with foil to keep the moisture in.

Roast the turkey in the preheated oven for about 30-40 minutes. Cooking times may vary depending on the size and thickness of the turkey.

Once cooked, remove the turkey from the oven and let it cool.

Slice or shred the turkey into small, bite-sized pieces suitable for your dog's size and preference.

Serve the roasted turkey as a main dish or mix it with your dog's regular food for added flavor and variety.

Ground Beef

Beef! Heck yeah! Just the thought of it has tails wagging around the world. Ground Beef is a super versatile meal base that'll make your pup's day—whether served on its own or mixed in with their favorite ingredients. Cook it up thoroughly, drain the extra fat, and watch your dog give you the *you're the best chef ever* look.

Ingredients

1 pound lean ground beef

1 tablespoon beef tallow or coconut oil

Directions

Heat a skillet or frying pan over medium heat and add the beef tallow or coconut oil.

Add the lean ground beef to the skillet and break it up using a spatula or spoon.

Cook the ground beef, stirring occasionally, until it is browned and fully cooked. This usually takes about 8-10 minutes.

Drain any excess fat from the cooked ground beef.

Let the beef cool, then serve it on its own for a protein-packed snack, or mix it with their favorite ingredients for a hearty meal that'll earn you some serious puppy-love points.

Safe Salmon Feeding Tips for Your Pup

- **Cooked Only:** Always serve cooked salmon to avoid harmful bacteria and parasites.

- **Choose Wild-Caught:** Opt for wild-caught salmon, which is more nutritious and lower in contaminants than farmed.

- **Remove Bones & Skin:** Debone and skin the salmon to prevent choking and digestive issues.

- **Keep It Plain:** Avoid seasonings, salt, and sauces, as they can be harmful to dogs.

- **Feed in Moderation:** Salmon is rich in omega-3s but should be given in moderation to prevent stomach upset and other health issues.

Wild Alaskan Salmon Filet

Get ready for the ultimate treat. "Wild" is the key here—this premium salmon is packed with Omega-3s and free from the contaminants often found in farm-raised or Pacific options. Just be sure to diligently remove all the bones for a safe, tail-wagging meal. With this filet, your pup's dinner is about to go gourmet.

Ingredients

2 wild-Alaskan salmon filets

1 tablespoon olive oil

1 tablespoon chopped fresh dill

Directions

Preheat your oven to 350°F (175°C) and line a baking sheet with parchment paper.

Place the wild-Alaskan salmon filets on the prepared baking sheet.

Drizzle olive oil over the filets, ensuring they are evenly coated.

Sprinkle the chopped fresh dill over the filets, pressing it gently into the flesh.

Place the baking sheet with the salmon in the preheated oven.

Bake for about 12-15 minutes, or until the salmon is opaque and flakes easily with a fork. The exact cooking time may vary depending on the thickness of the filets.

Once cooked, remove the salmon from the oven and let it cool. Make sure all bones and skin are removed.

Cut the salmon into bite-sized pieces for your pup, and consider serving it with a spoonful of Quinoa or Sweet Potato Mash (see The Basics section for recipes). This gourmet feast is fit for a four-legged foodie!

Mashed Sweet Potatoes

Get ready to whip up some Mashed Sweet Potatoes that are as tasty as they are nutritious for your furry friend. Not only are these sweet spuds delicious, but they are also packed with lots of nutrients. Boiling them helps keep all of those nutrients intact, though roasting is a fun alternative if you're feeling fancy.

With a treasure trove of vitamin A for a shiny coat and healthy skin, plus a rich supply of vitamins C, B6, potassium, calcium, and iron, these mashed delights are the perfect treat for pups and humans alike.

Ingredients

2 medium-sized sweet potatoes, diced

Directions

Wash the sweet potatoes thoroughly to remove dirt. Peel them if needed for easier digestion, or leave the skin on for added nutrients.

Cut into cubes or slices, then place in a pot with enough water to cover them completely. Bring to a boil over medium heat and then reduce the heat to low. Simmer for 10–15 minutes until tender.

Check doneness with a fork—it should slide in easily. Let cool before mashing into a smooth consistency or serve as bite-sized pieces.

Rice

Rice is the ultimate comfort food, serving as the fluffy foundation for so many delicious dishes. Whether you go for white or brown, both have their perks—brown rice is a low-glycemic superstar that won't send your pup's blood sugar soaring, while white rice is your go-to for calming upset tummies. Just remember to cook it thoroughly and skip the frying, and always serve it in moderation—because even the best treats deserve a little restraint.

Ingredients

1 cup of brown or white rice

2 cups of water or low-sodium chicken broth

Directions

Rinse the rice under cold water to remove excess starch.

In a saucepan, combine the rinsed rice with water or low-sodium chicken broth.

Bring to a boil over medium-high heat, then reduce heat to low, cover, and simmer—40–45 minutes for brown rice, 15–20 minutes for white rice—until tender.

Remove from heat and let sit, covered, for 5–10 minutes.

Fluff with a fork before serving. Serve plain or mix with cooked meat and vegetables.

Let cool before serving and using in other recipes.

Rice: A Gentle Comfort for Pups

Rice is a gentle and easily digestible carbohydrate source for dogs. It's important to cook the rice fully to make it easier for your dog to digest.

Quinoa

Quinoa is the superhero of grains—err, seeds—that brings a nutritious punch to your dog's diet. Packed with protein, fiber, and essential nutrients, this tiny powerhouse will have your pup feeling like they can leap tall fences in a single bound.

Ingredients

1 cup of quinoa

2 cups of water or low-sodium vegetable broth

Directions

Rinse the quinoa thoroughly under cold water to remove any bitter coating called saponin.

In a saucepan, combine the rinsed quinoa and water or vegetable broth.

Bring the mixture to a boil over medium-high heat.

Once boiling, reduce the heat to low and cover the saucepan with a lid.

Simmer the quinoa for about 15-20 minutes, or until all the liquid is absorbed and the quinoa is cooked.

Remove the saucepan from the heat and let the quinoa sit, covered, for 5 minutes.

Fluff the quinoa with a fork and let cool before serving it to your dog.

Homemade Pumpkin Puree

Get ready to bring a little pumpkin magic to your kitchen with Homemade Pumpkin Puree. Grab some sugar pumpkins or pie pumpkins for this delicious dish since they're sweeter and smoother than the decorative ones. And remember, steer clear of canned pumpkin pie filling—your pup doesn't need all those added sugars and spices. With this fresh puree, you'll have the perfect base for all kinds of tasty treats that will have your furry friend howling for more.

Ingredients

1 small pumpkin (sugar pumpkin or pie pumpkin)

1/4 teaspoon of ground cinnamon

Directions

Preheat your oven to 350°F (175°C).

Using a sharp knife, carefully cut the pumpkin in half vertically.

Scoop out the seeds and pulp from the center of the pumpkin using a spoon or ice cream scoop.

Place the pumpkin halves, cut side down, on a baking sheet lined with parchment paper.

Bake the pumpkin in the preheated oven for about 45-60 minutes, or until the flesh is tender and easily pierced with a fork.

Remove the pumpkin from the oven and let it cool for a few minutes until it's safe to handle.

Once cooled, use a spoon to scoop out the roasted flesh from the pumpkin halves.

Transfer the pumpkin flesh to a food processor or blender. Add the ground cinnamon.

Blend or process the pumpkin and cinnamon until it reaches a smooth and creamy consistency. You can add a small amount of water if needed to help with blending.

Allow the pumpkin puree to cool completely before using.

Applesauce

Whip up a batch of homemade applesauce that's so tasty, your pup will think it's dessert. Packed with sweet, juicy apples and just a dash of cinnamon, it's the perfect treat for adding a little fruity flair to snack time—or even drizzling over their favorite meals.

Ingredients

2-3 medium-sized apples (Gala or Fuji)

Water for boiling (enough to cover the apples)

Sprinkle of cinnamon

Directions

Wash the apples thoroughly and remove the cores, seeds, and stems. You can peel the apples or leave the skin on, depending on your preference.

Cut the apples into small chunks to speed up the cooking process and ensure they cook evenly.

Place the apple chunks in a medium-sized saucepan and add enough water to cover them.

Bring the water to a boil over medium heat and then reduce the heat to low. Let the apples simmer for about 15-20 minutes or until they are soft and easily mashed with a fork.

Remove the saucepan from the heat and allow the cooked apples to cool slightly.

Mash the apples using a fork, or for a smoother consistency, blend them in a food processor or blender. If desired, you can add a sprinkle of cinnamon for added flavor.

Let the applesauce cool completely before serving it to your dog.

Special Occasions

Special moments deserve a grand celebration! Whether it's a birthday bash, a festive holiday, or even your dog throwing a neighborhood puppy play date on Friday, why not roll out the red carpet with some tail-wagging treats? Your furry friend will feel like the superstar they are, and let's be honest, who doesn't love a reason to indulge?

Barkuterie Board

This Barkuterie Board isn't just a snack—it's a full-blown party on a plate, guaranteed to get tails wagging and your pup's friends howling with joy. Create a paw-sitively delightful board filled with a variety of dog-friendly treats like fruits, vegetables, meats, and cheeses. For an extra touch, arrange the items in the shape of a paw to score some serious style points. Your dog and their friends will be amazed at your creativity and talent!

Here's a list of ideas to get you started:

Apples

Applesauce (see The Basics chapter for recipe)

Carrots

Cheddar cheese, low-fat (cut into small cubes)

Chicken breast, shredded

Crackers (see Special Occasions chapter for recipe)

Cucumbers

Green and red peppers

Mozzarella (cut into small cubes)

Peanut Butter Yogurt Dip (see Special Occasions chapter for recipe)

Pumpkin Puree (see The Basics chapter for recipe)

Pumpkin and Cottage Cheese Dip (see Special Occasions chapter for recipe)

Squash

Turkey, roasted and shredded (see The Basics chapter for recipe)

Watermelon

Zucchini

Directions

Choose your dog's favorite foods and wash, slice, and prep as needed. Cook and cool any meats, then dice or shred them. Arrange fruits, veggies, cheeses, and meats on a dog-safe platter. Add small bowls of dips and crackers for variety. Finish by filling any gaps with bite-sized treats. Get creative and have fun!

Why Deli Meats Are a No-Go for Pups

Stay clear of deli meats. They are often high in sodium, which can lead to dehydration and electrolyte imbalances in dogs. They can also be heavily processed and may contain harmful additives, preservatives, and seasonings. They may contain common allergens such as wheat, soy, or artificial additives that can cause allergic reactions or digestive issues.

Peanut Butter Yogurt Dip

This dreamy dip combines creamy peanut butter and velvety yogurt for a deliciously paw-some treat that'll have your pup licking the bowl clean. My dog Lewie was peanut butter's biggest fan. I can picture him drooling in anticipation!

Ingredients

1/2 cup plain yogurt

2 tablespoons natural peanut butter (unsalted, no added sugars)

Directions

In a small bowl, mix the yogurt and peanut butter until well combined.

Serve as a dip for dog-friendly fruits or vegetables like apple slices, carrot sticks, or celery.

Pumpkin and Cottage Cheese Dip

Get ready for a creamy delight that mixes sweet pumpkin with smooth cottage cheese, creating a dip so tasty your pup will be begging for every last lick.

Ingredients

1/2 cup pumpkin puree

1/4 cup low-fat cottage cheese

Directions

In a bowl, mix the pumpkin puree and cottage cheese until well blended.

Serve as a dip for dog-friendly biscuits, or use a dollop on top of meals or treats.

Puree Your Way: Homemade or Canned

Want to make your own Homemade Pumpkin Puree? Check out The Basics chapter for a simple, step-by-step recipe. If you're short on time, canned unsweetened puree works just as well—just make sure it's pure pumpkin with no added sugars or spices.

Homemade Crackers

These delightful little bites are crunchy, wholesome, and made with love. Perfect for a barkuterie board and dips.

Ingredients

1 cup whole wheat flour

1/4 cup rolled oats

1/4 cup finely grated carrots or sweet potatoes

1/4 cup unsweetened applesauce (see The Basics chapter)

1/4 cup low-sodium chicken or vegetable broth

Directions

Preheat your oven to 350°F (175°C) and line a baking sheet with parchment paper.

In a mixing bowl, combine the whole wheat flour and rolled oats.

Add the grated carrots or sweet potatoes to the dry ingredients and mix well.

Add the unsweetened applesauce to the bowl and mix until the ingredients are well combined.

Gradually add the chicken or vegetable broth while mixing, until the dough comes together and forms a ball.

Lightly flour a clean surface and roll out the dough to about 1/4-inch thickness.

Use a cookie cutter or a knife to cut out small shapes or squares from the dough.

Place the cut-out crackers onto the prepared baking sheet.

Bake in the preheated oven for about 20-25 minutes, or until the crackers are golden and crispy.

Allow the crackers to cool completely before serving.

Birthday Cake

Hey, Mom and Dad, it's time to celebrate a birthday! This Birthday Cake will have your pup looking forward to their birthday every year. Jam packed with nutrients and outstanding flavor, this cake is guaranteed to be your furry friends favorite birthday present.

Ingredients

2 cups whole wheat flour

1 teaspoon baking powder

1/4 cup unsweetened applesauce

1/4 cup plain Greek yogurt

1/4 cup natural peanut butter (make sure it does not contain xylitol)

2 ripe bananas, mashed

2 eggs

1/2 cup water

Frosting:

1/2 cup plain Greek yogurt

1/4 cup unsalted, natural peanut butter (make sure it does not contain xylitol)

1 tablespoon honey

Directions

Preheat your oven to 350°F (175°C) and lightly grease a round cake pan.

In a large bowl, whisk together the whole wheat flour and baking powder.

In a separate bowl, mix together the applesauce, Greek yogurt, peanut butter, mashed bananas, eggs, and water until well combined.

Gradually add the wet ingredients to the dry ingredients, stirring until just combined. Be careful not to over mix.

Pour the batter into the prepared cake pan and smooth the top with a spatula.

Bake in the preheated oven for approximately 25-30 minutes, or until a toothpick inserted into the center comes out clean.

Remove the cake from the oven and let it cool completely.

In a bowl, combine the plain Greek yogurt and peanut butter.

Stir the ingredients together until well combined and smooth.

Taste the mixture and add honey if a touch of sweetness is desired.

Once the frosting is ready, you can spread it on top of the cooled cake using a spatula or piping bag. And as a special treat, you can let your dog lick the frosting directly from the spoon.

Frosting Fun—In Moderation

Frosting is intended as a special treat, so remember to give it in moderation. Want to make it extra special? Decorate the frosted cake with some dog-friendly treats! For more Decoration Ideas, check out the Special Occasions chapter.

Decoration Ideas

Decorations for dogs are the sprinkles on the cupcake of mealtime—because why shouldn't their dishes be as beautiful as they are tasty? A little garnish here and a colorful topping there can transform an ordinary bowl into a culinary masterpiece, making every meal feel like a special occasion worthy of tail wags and puppy kisses!

Here are some fun toppings to put the finishing touches on meals and desserts that will make your dog drool:

Dog Biscuits or Treats: Crush or finely chop dog-friendly treats to sprinkle over frosting or around the edges of cakes, pupcakes, or meals for added texture and an extra layer of flavor. Alternatively, use whole biscuits or themed treats as decorative toppers or to line the edges of desserts or main dishes.

Dog-Safe Herbs: Sprinkle some finely chopped dog-safe herbs like parsley, mint or cilantro on top of your dog's food. Not only do they add a burst of freshness, but they can also provide some additional health benefits.

Freeze-Dried Meat or Fish: Break small pieces of freeze-dried meat or fish treats and use them as decorative accents. They add flavor, texture, and a visually appealing touch to treats and meals.

Fresh Fruit: Dogs can enjoy many fruits in moderation. Decorate with slices of dog-safe fruits like apples, blueberries, strawberries, or watermelon. Just make sure to remove any seeds, pits, or rinds that could be harmful.

Shredded Carrots or Coconut: Add a sprinkle of shredded carrots or coconut on top of cakes or meals for a visually appealing touch.

Veggie Sprinkles: Finely chop dog-safe vegetables like carrots, zucchini, or green beans and sprinkle them on top of your dog's food or treats. This adds a pop of color and extra nutrients.

Whipped Cream: Use a small dollop of unsweetened, lactose-free whipped cream as a decorative element. Dogs generally enjoy the taste and texture but remember to use it sparingly and avoid whipped cream with added sugars or artificial sweeteners.

Paw-some Snacks

When it comes to healthy snacks for dogs, think outside the kibble. Give them nutritious snacks to keep your dog's chompers busy. Just remember: everything in moderation...unless you enjoy extra wagging and puppy eyes begging for more.

Carrot and Cheese Muffins

These muffins are the ulti-mutt treat, combining cheesy goodness with nutritious carrots for a snack that'll have your pup sitting, staying, and drooling for more.

Ingredients

2 cups grated carrots

1 cup shredded cheddar cheese

1/4 cup coconut flour

3 eggs

Directions

Preheat the oven to 350°F (175°C) and line a muffin tin with paper liners.

In a bowl, mix together the grated carrots, shredded cheddar cheese, coconut flour, and eggs until well combined.

Spoon the batter into the prepared muffin tin, filling each cup about 3/4 full.

Bake for 20-25 minutes or until a toothpick inserted into the center comes out clean.

Let the muffins cool completely before serving them to your happy dog whose been waiting patiently by the oven for what seems to be an eternity.

Sweet Potato and Chickpea Bites

Imagine little nuggets of doggy bliss—wholesome, tasty, and perfect for pups who crave a seriously delicious snack! These bites pack a flavor punch that will have your furry friend begging for more.

Ingredients

1 large sweet potato, cooked and mashed

1 cup canned chickpeas (drained and rinsed), mashed

1/4 cup oat flour (you can make your own by grinding oats in a blender)

1 tablespoon ground flaxseed mixed with 3 tablespoons water (as an egg substitute)

1 tablespoon olive oil

Directions

Prepare the sweet potato as directed in The Basics chapter.

Rinse canned chickpeas in cold water and mash. If you need to soften, boil for 5 minutes in water with a small amount of baking soda.

Preheat the oven to 350°F (175°C) and line a baking sheet with parchment paper.

In a mixing bowl, combine the mashed sweet potato, mashed chickpeas, oat flour, flaxseed mixture, and olive oil. Mix well to form a dough-like consistency.

Scoop small portions of the mixture and roll them into bite-sized balls.

Place the balls on the prepared baking sheet.

Bake for about 25-30 minutes or until the bites are firm and lightly browned.

Serve these bites cool to the touch and watch your pup savor every nibble.

Applesauce Made Easy

Check The Basics chapter for step-by-step instructions on making homemade Applesauce. Fresh applesauce is rich in fiber and vitamins, making it a tasty and nutritious addition to your pup's treats. If you're short on time, store-bought applesauce works too—just make sure it's unsweetened with no added sugars or harmful ingredients.

Apple Cinnamon Biscuits

Who's a good human? You are! You'll get a gold star on the refrigerator from your dog when you make these delicious biscuits. These biscuits are like apple pie for pups, minus the guilt.

Ingredients

2 cups oat flour (or grind rolled oats in a blender or food processor)

1/2 cup unsweetened applesauce

1/4 cup natural almond butter (unsalted and unsweetened)

1 teaspoon ground cinnamon

1/2 teaspoon baking powder

1/4 cup finely grated apple (choose a dog-safe variety such as Granny Smith)

1 tablespoon honey (optional, for added sweetness)

Water (as needed)

Directions

Preheat your oven to 350°F (175°C) and line a baking sheet with parchment paper.

In a large mixing bowl, combine the oat flour, applesauce, almond butter, ground cinnamon, baking powder, finely grated apple, and honey (if using). Mix well until a dough forms. If the dough is too dry, add a small amount of water to achieve a workable consistency.

Lightly flour a clean surface, then roll out the dough to approximately 1/4-inch thickness.

Use fun shaped cookie cutters, such as hearts or bones, to cut out shapes from the dough and place them onto the prepared baking sheet.

Bake the biscuits in the preheated oven for about 15-20 minutes or until they turn golden brown and firm to the touch.

Let the biscuits cool completely on a wire rack and serve as a special treat or a reward after playtime. Serve with a small spoonful of unsweetened applesauce for a delightful dipping option.

Cheesy Broccoli Bites

Presenting the treat that lets your dog snack like a health nut while still thinking it's junk food. These bites are perfect for the pup who's all about wellness... or at least pretending to be between couch naps.

Ingredients

2 cups of broccoli florets

1 tablespoon of coconut oil

Sprinkle of nutritional yeast

Directions

Preheat the oven to 350°F (175°C) and line a baking sheet with parchment paper.

Wash the broccoli florets and cut them into small bite-sized pieces.

Toss the broccoli pieces with a small amount of melted coconut oil for added flavor and moisture. Add a sprinkle of nutritional yeast and mix well.

Spread the broccoli pieces evenly on the prepared baking sheet.

Bake in the preheated oven for about 15-20 minutes or until the broccoli is tender and slightly crispy.

Serve these broccoli bites cool as a crunchy, veggie-packed reward—perfect for snack time or after a fun play session.

Nutritional Yeast: A Cheesy Boost of Nutrition

Nutritional yeast isn't just delicious—it's packed with B vitamins that support your pup's energy levels and immune system. Its cheesy flavor makes it a great topping for treats, and the extra nutrients give your dog a healthy boost with every bite.

Peanut Butter and Pumpkin Balls

This treat combines your dog's two true loves—peanut butter and... pumpkin? Yup, it's like the canine version of a fancy fall snack, except they'll be inhaling these faster than you can say "good dog!"

Ingredients

1 cup canned pumpkin puree (unsweetened and plain)

1/2 cup natural peanut butter or almond butter (unsalted, no added sugar)

2 cups rolled oats

Directions

In a large bowl, mix together the pumpkin puree and peanut butter or almond butter.

Gradually add the rolled oats and stir until well combined.

Roll the mixture into bite-sized balls and place them on a baking sheet.

Chill the balls in the fridge for at least an hour until they're firm—then let the pup-approved snacking begin.

Meals To Warm The Heart

This is where doggy dreams come true. These meals are crafted to nourish and delight, giving your pup that cozy, cared-for feeling—because they deserve meals as warm and wonderful as the love they bring to your life. Get ready for empty bowls and thank-you snuggles.

Hawaiian Mackerel

Hawaiian Mackerel is the tropical escape your dog didn't know they needed. With flavorful mackerel and a hint of island-inspired ingredients, it's a beachy feast in a bowl that'll have them daydreaming of sandy paws and ocean breezes, even if they're just in the backyard.

Ingredients

1/2 pound mackerel filet, boneless and skinless

1/4 cup cooked and mashed sweet potatoes

1/4 cup cooked and chopped spinach

1/4 cup diced pineapple (fresh or canned in water, not syrup)

1 tablespoon chopped fresh cilantro

1 tablespoon coconut oil (optional)

Directions

Prepare the sweet potatoes as directed in The Basics chapter.

Preheat the oven to 375°F (190°C).

Place the mackerel filet on a baking sheet lined with parchment paper.

Bake the mackerel in the oven for approximately 15-20 minutes, or until it is thoroughly cooked through and flakes easily with a fork. Let it cool.

Once cooled, carefully remove all bones from the mackerel to ensure it is safe for your pup.

In a bowl, flake the cooked mackerel into small pieces using a fork.

Add the mashed sweet potatoes, chopped spinach, diced pineapple, chopped cilantro, and coconut oil (if using) to the bowl with the mackerel.

Mix all the ingredients together until well combined.

Serve the Hawaiian mackerel mixture as a topper for your dog's regular meal or as a standalone treat—get ready for happy tail wags and a very satisfied pup.

Shepherd's Pie

Brace yourselves for a hearty, meaty, veggie-packed masterpiece that'll have your dog convinced they're dining like a royal shepherd.

Ingredients

1/2 cup cooked and mashed sweet potatoes

1/4 cup cooked peas

1/4 cup cooked carrots (finely chopped or mashed)

1 cup cooked ground turkey or chicken

1/4 cup low-sodium chicken broth

Directions

Preheat your oven to 350°F (175°C).

Prepare the sweet potatoes as directed in The Basics chapter.

Steam or boil the peas and carrots until soft. Drain and set aside to cool.

In a pan, cook the ground turkey or chicken until fully cooked and no longer pink.

In a mixing bowl, combine the cooked ground turkey or chicken, mashed sweet potatoes, cooked peas, and cooked carrots.

Add the chicken broth to the mixture and stir well to combine all the ingredients. The broth helps create moisture in the dish.

Transfer the mixture into a small baking dish.

Bake in the preheated oven for about 15-20 minutes, or until the top is lightly browned and the ingredients are heated through.

Let the Shepherd's Pie cool down completely, then do a quick heat check—your pup will love every bite when it's just the right temperature.

Mexican Taco Bowl

It's fiesta in a bowl that'll have your pup ready to salsa and saying "muy delicioso".

Ingredients

1/2 pound lean ground turkey

1/4 cup canned black beans

1/4 cup cooked and diced sweet potatoes

1 tablespoon chopped fresh cilantro

Directions

Prepare the sweet potatoes as directed in The Basics chapter.

In a pan, cook the ground turkey until no longer pink and fully cooked. Drain any excess fat and let it cool.

In a bowl, mix together the black beans, diced sweet potatoes, cooked ground turkey, and cilantro until well combined.

Serve up this delicious taco bowl and watch your pup dive in for a fiesta of flavors—tail dancing guaranteed.

Cilantro: A Detox Powerhouse

Cilantro is known for its detoxifying properties, helping to remove heavy metals from the body. It's also rich in vitamins A and K, promoting a healthy immune system. Add a little cilantro to brighten up their bowl and boost nutrition.

Beef and Veggie Stir-Fry

Here's a savory, sizzlin' meal that'll have your pup drooling before it even hits the bowl. Loaded with tender beef and crunchy veggies, it's a stir-fry so good, your dog might start giving you that "where's my chopsticks?" look.

Ingredients

1/2-pound lean beef, thinly sliced

1 cup mixed vegetables (carrots, broccoli, and bell peppers), chopped

1 tablespoon olive oil

1/2 teaspoon ginger powder

1/2 teaspoon turmeric powder

1/2 cup cooked brown rice or quinoa (optional)

Directions

If using, prepare the rice or quinoa as directed in The Basics chapter.

Heat the olive oil in a large skillet or wok over medium-high heat.

Add the thinly sliced beef to the skillet and cook until browned and cooked through. Remove the beef from the skillet and set it aside.

In the same skillet, add the chopped vegetables and stir-fry them for a few minutes until they are tender-crisp.

Add in the ginger and turmeric to coat the vegetables.

Return the cooked beef to the skillet and toss it with the vegetables to combine.

Once cooled, mix the beef and veggie stir-fry with a small portion of brown rice or quinoa for an extra filling meal that is comforting and easy to digest.

Spoon out this delicious beef and veggie stir-fry, and watch your furry friend dig in with pure delight.

Turkey and Pumpkin Stew

Think of this as Thanksgiving in a bowl—minus the family drama, but with all the tail-wagging joy. With savory turkey and creamy pumpkin, it's like a holiday celebration in every bite.

Ingredients

1 cup cooked ground turkey

1 tablespoon olive oil

1/4 cup cooked quinoa or rice

1/2 cup pumpkin puree (unsweetened and plain)

1/4 cup chopped green beans

1 cup low-sodium chicken broth

Directions

Prepare the quinoa or rice as directed in The Basics chapter.

In a pan, heat the olive oil over medium heat. Cook the ground turkey until fully cooked and no longer pink. Drain any excess fat and let it cool.

In a saucepan, combine the cooked ground turkey, pumpkin puree, cooked quinoa or rice, chopped green beans, and chicken broth.

Stir well and bring the mixture to a simmer over medium heat.

Reduce the heat to low and let the stew cook for about 10-15 minutes, allowing the flavors to blend.

Remove from heat and let the stew cool before serving it to your dog.

Scoop the stew into your dog's bowl, and watch them dig in with pure joy— it's a wholesome meal they'll love to the last drop.

Pumpkin Puree Tips

For Homemade Pumpkin Puree, see The Basics chapter for easy instructions. If using canned, choose plain, unsweetened puree. Avoid pumpkin pie filling—it often contains nutmeg, which is toxic, and added sugar, which is unhealthy for your pup.

Poke Bowl

Imagine a sunny beach, waves gently lapping at the shore—this tropical-inspired poke bowl is a taste of paradise, minus the sand on your paws and the cost of airfare.

Ingredients

1/2 cup cooked salmon or tuna, diced (without bones)

1/4 cup cooked brown rice or quinoa

1/4 cup cucumber, diced

1/4 cup carrot, shredded

1/4 cup green beans, steamed and chopped

1/4 cup pineapple, diced

1 tablespoon plain Greek yogurt

1/2 teaspoon coconut oil, melted

1/2 teaspoon seaweed flakes (nori or dulse, free from seasoning)

Directions

Prepare the salmon and quinoa or rice as directed in The Basics chapter.

In a dog-friendly bowl, combine the cooked and diced salmon or tuna (bones removed), cooked brown rice or quinoa, cucumber, carrot, green beans, and pineapple.

Add the plain Greek yogurt to the bowl and mix it with the ingredients for added creaminess.

Drizzle the coconut oil over the ingredients and sprinkle the seaweed flakes on top.

Gently toss the ingredients to combine everything well.

Scoop the Poke Bowl into a colorful bowl, and serve it to your pup at room temperature for a taste of paradise that'll have them drooling.

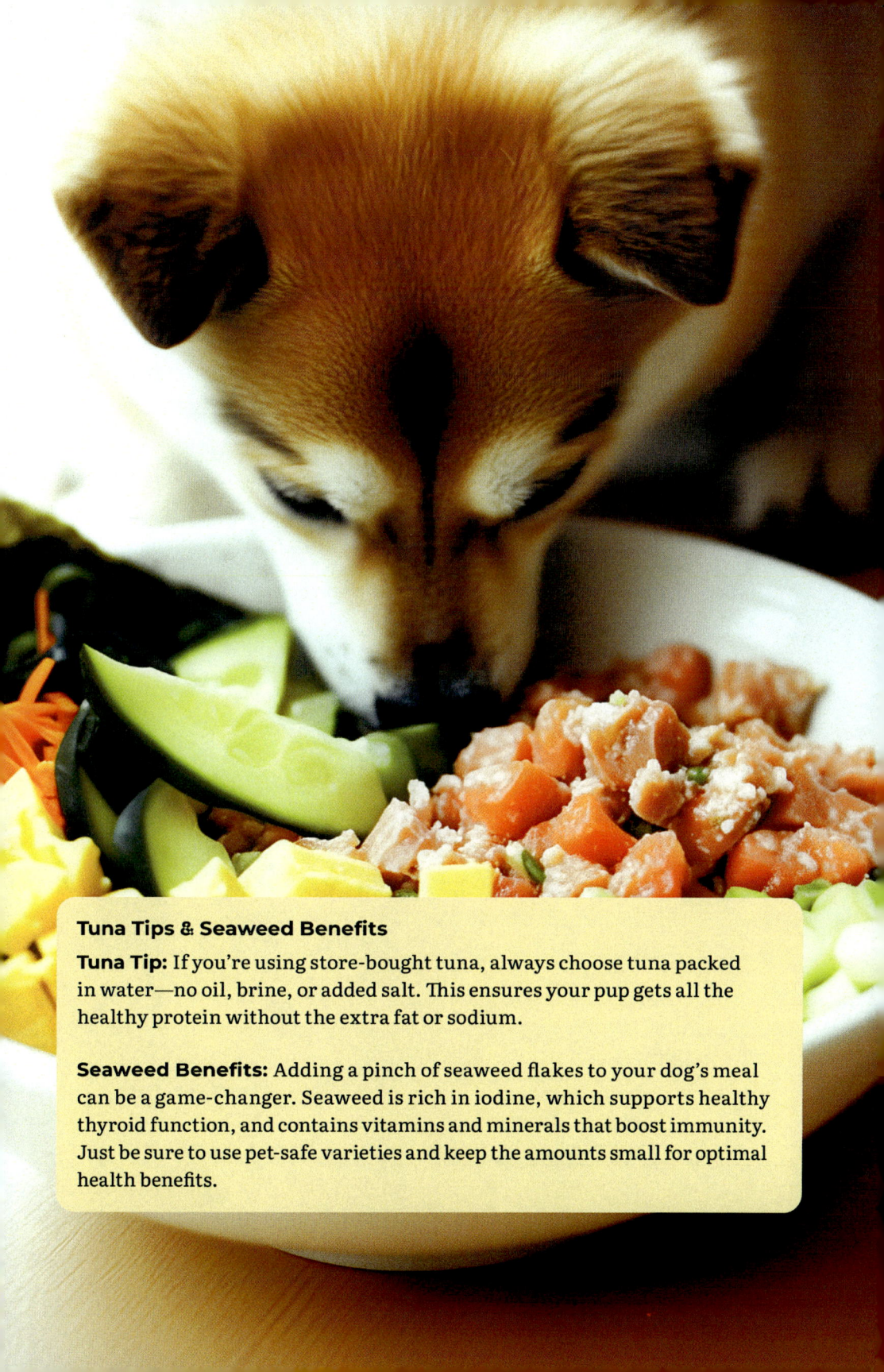

Tuna Tips & Seaweed Benefits

Tuna Tip: If you're using store-bought tuna, always choose tuna packed in water—no oil, brine, or added salt. This ensures your pup gets all the healthy protein without the extra fat or sodium.

Seaweed Benefits: Adding a pinch of seaweed flakes to your dog's meal can be a game-changer. Seaweed is rich in iodine, which supports healthy thyroid function, and contains vitamins and minerals that boost immunity. Just be sure to use pet-safe varieties and keep the amounts small for optimal health benefits.

Salmon and Sweet Potato Patties

Spoil your sweet four-legged friend with savory salmon and velvety sweet potato patties. Perfect for pups who deserve a little extra pampering with every bite.

Ingredients

1 cup cooked salmon, flaked, bones removed

1 cup cooked sweet potato, mashed

1/4 cup oat flour (or finely ground oats)

1 egg, beaten

Directions

Prepare the salmon and sweet potato as directed in The Basics chapter.

In a bowl, combine the cooked salmon (ensuring all bones are removed), mashed sweet potato, oat flour, and beaten egg.

Mix well until all the ingredients are thoroughly combined.

Shape the mixture into small patties and place them on a greased baking sheet.

Bake at 350°F (175°C) for 20-25 minutes or until cooked through.

Allow the patties to cool before serving it to your dog.

Dish it out, and prepare for some happy tail-wagging and big puppy grins.

Turkey and Vegetable Meatloaf

Your dog is already drooling at the thought of juicy turkey and veggies—and who could blame them? This dish brings all the cozy vibes of a Sunday roast, complete with the warm, comforting flavors they love. Don't be surprised if those irresistible puppy eyes come out, practically begging for seconds (and maybe even thirds).

Ingredients

1 pound ground turkey

1/2 cup grated zucchini

1/4 cup grated carrot

1/4 cup oat flour (or finely ground oats)

1 egg, beaten

Directions

Preheat the oven to 350°F (175°C) and line a loaf pan with parchment paper for easy cleanup.

In a bowl, mix together the ground turkey, grated zucchini, grated carrot, oat flour, and beaten egg.

Transfer the mixture to the prepared loaf pan and press it down evenly.

Bake for 40-45 minutes or until cooked through.

Let the meatloaf cool before slicing it into appropriate portions for your dog.

Spoon into your pup's bowl and get ready for a drool-worthy reaction.

Gravy for Extra Tail Wags!

Add a drizzle of dog-safe gravy on top for an extra special treat. It's the perfect way to make mealtime feel like a celebration—because every pup deserves a little extra love now and then. Find the Easy Gravy recipe in The Basics chapter to whip up this delicious topper.

Berry-licious Chicken Salad

Brimming with tender chicken and juicy blueberries, this refreshing salad is a flavor-packed treat that'll have your dog wondering if they've become a true culinary connoisseur. It's light, tasty, and bursting with goodness—perfect for the pup with a taste for the finer things in life.

Ingredients

1 cup cooked chicken breast, shredded

1/2 cup blueberries

1/4 cup diced cucumber

1/4 cup diced watermelon

1 tablespoon plain Greek yogurt

1 tablespoon chopped fresh mint

Directions

Prepare the chicken breast as directed in The Basics chapter.

In a bowl, combine the cooked shredded chicken breast, blueberries, cucumber, and watermelon. Mix well.

Stir in the plain Greek yogurt for added creaminess.

Serve the salad with a small garnish of mint for a fresh twist that adds some fun to your dog's dining experience.

Blueberries: Nature's Super Snack

Blueberries are a perfect bite-sized treat for your pup. Packed with antioxidants, fiber, and vitamins C and K, they help support your dog's immune system and promote overall health. Plus, they're naturally sweet—your dog will love them as a healthy snack or meal topper!

Lamb and Couscous Pilaf

With savory lamb and fluffy couscous, this pilaf is a bowl of cozy flavors your pup won't be able to resist. It's a little taste of the Mediterranean, crafted just for them. Get ready for happy munching and maybe even a fancy head tilt of approval.

Ingredients

1 pound lamb, cut into small pieces

1 tablespoon olive oil

1 cup low-sodium chicken or vegetable broth

1 cup couscous

1 teaspoon ground cumin

1 teaspoon ground coriander

1/2 teaspoon turmeric

Salt and pepper, to taste

1 teaspoon plain unsweetened yogurt

Chopped fresh parsley or cilantro, for garnish

Directions

In a large skillet or pan, heat the olive oil over medium heat. Add the lamb pieces and cook until browned on all sides. Remove the lamb from the skillet and set aside.

In a saucepan, boil the chicken or vegetable broth. Add the couscous to the pan and stir to combine with the ground cumin, ground coriander, and turmeric to the pan. You can add a small amount of salt and pepper to taste.

Bring the mixture back to a boil, then reduce the heat to low. Cover the pan and simmer for about 10-15 minutes, or until the couscous is cooked and the liquid is absorbed.

Once the couscous is cooked, return the lamb to the pan and stir to combine with the pilaf.

Remove from heat and let the pilaf sit, covered, for a few minutes to allow the flavors to meld together.

Serve the lamb pilaf cooled and mix in a teaspoon of plain, unsweetened yogurt for extra creaminess. Garnished with chopped fresh parsley or cilantro for extra flavor and nutrients.

Dish it out and brace yourself for some serious puppy appreciation.

Cumin: A Flavorful Boost for Your Pup

Cumin isn't just a tasty spice—it's a nutritional powerhouse! It can aid digestion, support the immune system, and has natural anti-inflammatory properties, making it a great addition to your dog's diet. Just remember, a small pinch is enough to add flavor and health benefits without overwhelming your pup's sensitive palate.

Tasty Treats for the Goodest Boys and Girls

Got a pup with a bit of a sweet tooth? These homemade treats are deliciously free from added sugars and preservatives, making snack time healthier (even if your dog thinks they should get the whole batch!).

Remember, treats are like a little sprinkle of love—but in this case, love should be served in small doses (though try explaining that to those puppy eyes…).

Blueberry and Oat Bars

Packed with juicy blueberries and wholesome oats, this treat is like a breakfast bar for your best buddy. One bite, and your pup will be ready for adventure—or maybe just a cozy nap.

Ingredients

1 cup fresh or frozen blueberries

1 cup rolled oats

1/2 cup unsweetened applesauce (see The Basics chapter for recipe)

2 tablespoons honey

Directions

Preheat the oven to 350°F (175°C) and line a baking dish with parchment paper.

In a bowl, combine the blueberries, rolled oats, applesauce, and honey.

Mix well until all the ingredients are evenly distributed.

Transfer the mixture to the prepared baking dish and spread it out evenly.

Bake for 25-30 minutes or until golden brown.

Let the bars cool completely before cutting them into smaller pieces for serving. Be prepared for some grateful, excited barks.

Banana and Carrot Pupcakes

It's pupcake time! These Banana and Carrot Pupcakes are the perfect treat to make any dog feel like the guest of honor. With a sweet banana base and carrot bits mixed in, they're like a little slice of doggie heaven—paw-lickin' good and ruff-tastically delicious.

Ingredients

1 ripe banana, mashed

1/2 cup grated carrots

1/4 cup coconut flour

2 tablespoons natural peanut butter (unsalted, no added sugars)

2 eggs

Directions

Preheat the oven to 350°F (175°C) and line a muffin tin with paper liners.

In a bowl, mix together the mashed banana, grated carrots, coconut flour, peanut butter, and eggs until well combined.

Spoon the batter into the prepared muffin tin, filling each cup about 3/4 full.

Bake for 20-25 minutes or until a toothpick inserted into the center comes out clean.

Serve cooled for a delightful pupcake treat—perfect for celebrating any moment with your furry friend.

More Deliciousness Please

Want to make your pup's special day even better? Add a dog-safe peanut butter drizzle on top of their pupcake, and watch those tails wag! You can also sprinkle with a few blueberries or a dollop of plain yogurt to add a little flair.

Peanut Butter and Oatmeal Cookies

Imagine this: you and your dog catch a whiff of peanut butter, and suddenly, it's like you've found the treasure at the end of the rainbow. These chewy bites have oats to sweeten the deal. You'd sit, stay, and maybe even roll over for one of these treats... if that's what it takes.

Ingredients

1 1/2 cups rolled oats

1/2 cup unsalted and unsweetened peanut butter

1 ripe banana, mashed

1 tablespoon ground flaxseed

Water, as needed

Directions

Preheat the oven to 350°F (175°C) and line a baking sheet with parchment paper.

In a mixing bowl, combine the rolled oats, peanut butter, mashed banana, and ground flaxseed. Mix well until the ingredients are thoroughly combined.

Add water gradually, a tablespoon at a time, until the mixture comes together and forms a dough. The dough should be slightly sticky but manageable.

On a lightly floured surface, roll out the dough to about 1/4-inch thickness.

Use cookie cutters to cut out shapes or simply use a knife to cut the dough into small squares.

Place the treats onto the prepared baking sheet.

Bake for about 15-20 minutes or until the treats are golden brown and firm.

Remove from the oven and let them cool completely on a wire rack.

Once cooled, serve with love, and watch your furry friend devour it like it's the best meal of their life.

Wild Alaskan Salmon Cookies

Ready to spoil your little "wolf of the wild"? These rich in omega-3 and protein Wild Alaskan Salmon Cookies will have them believing they've just reeled in a fresh catch. They'll be howling for more.

Ingredients

1 cup cooked and flaked wild-Alaskan salmon (boneless, skinless)

1/2 cup cooked and mashed sweet potato

1/4 cup coconut flour (or whole wheat flour as an alternative)

1/4 cup rolled oats

1 egg, beaten

Directions

Prepare the salmon and sweet potatoes by following the recipe in The Basics chapter of this book. Be sure to carefully remove all bones from the salmon to ensure it is safe for your pup.

Preheat your oven to 350°F (175°C) and line a baking sheet with parchment paper.

In a mixing bowl, combine the flaked salmon, mashed sweet potato, coconut flour, rolled oats, and beaten egg.

Stir the ingredients together until they are well combined and form a thick dough.

Roll the dough into small balls or use a cookie cutter to create desired shapes.

Place the shaped treats onto the prepared baking sheet, leaving a bit of space between them.

Flatten the treats slightly with the back of a fork or your hand.

Bake in the preheated oven for about 15-20 minutes, or until the treats are firm and golden.

Remove from the oven and let the treats cool completely on a wire rack.

Serve these treats cool, and watch your pup gobble them up like they're at an all-you-can-eat seafood buffet— tail wags guaranteed.

Fur-eeze: Frozen Doggie Delights

Here's the coolest collection of treats for hot days and happy pups! From fruity pupsicles to creamy delights, these frosty recipes are perfect for keeping tails wagging all summer long. Just be warned: one taste, and your pup might become best friends with the freezer.

Berry Banana Smoothie

Get ready for a fruity fiesta your pup won't be able to resist. This blend of juicy berries and creamy banana is the ultimate refreshing treat, packed with natural sweetness and a boost of vitamins. One lick, and your dog will feel like they're living the good life.

Ingredients

1/2 cup frozen mixed berries (blueberries, strawberries, raspberries)

1 ripe banana

1/2 cup plain Greek yogurt

1/4 cup unsweetened coconut water

Directions

Place the frozen mixed berries, ripe banana, Greek yogurt, and coconut water in a blender.

Blend on high speed until all the ingredients are well combined and the smoothie has a smooth consistency.

Serve the smoothie in a small bowl or use it to fill a dog-safe ice cube tray. Freeze the cubes and let your dog enjoy a cool, berry-packed treat on a hot day.

Banana Bonus: Freeze Now, Smoothie Later

Got an overly ripe banana? Pop it in the freezer and save it for later— frozen bananas make any smoothie extra creamy and delicious!

Banana Peanut Butter Ice Cream

Get ready for a swirl of happiness. It's the perfect creamy blend of sweet banana and nutty peanut butter, guaranteed to make your pup's tail go into overdrive. Don't be surprised if they beat you to the freezer.

Ingredients

2 ripe bananas

2 tablespoons unsalted and unsweetened peanut butter (make sure it does not contain xylitol)

1/2 cup unsweetened coconut milk

Directions

Peel the bananas and cut them into small pieces.

Place the banana pieces in a freezer bag or container and freeze them for a few hours or overnight until they are completely frozen.

Once the bananas are frozen, remove them from the freezer and let them sit at room temperature for a few minutes to soften slightly.

In a blender or food processor, combine the frozen banana pieces, peanut butter, and coconut milk.

Blend the mixture until smooth and creamy.

Pour the mixture into a bowl or ice cream molds.

Place the bowl or molds in the freezer and allow the ice cream to set for at least 2 hours or until firm.

Once the ice cream is fully frozen, scoop out the ice cream and watch your pup dive in like they've just discovered their own secret stash of dessert heaven.

Mango Coconut Sorbet

Turn up the tropical vibes with this icy mango-coconut treat! It's a refreshing blend of fruity goodness that'll make your pup feel like they're lounging on a beach—pawfect for cooling down on those sunny days.

Ingredients

2 ripe mangoes, peeled and pitted

1/2 cup coconut milk (unsweetened)

1/4 cup plain Greek yogurt (unsweetened)

1 tablespoon honey

1/4 cup shredded unsweetened coconut

Directions

Cut the ripe mangoes into small pieces and place them in a blender or food processor.

Add the coconut milk, plain Greek yogurt, and honey to the blender or food processor.

Blend the ingredients until smooth and well combined.

Add the shredded unsweetened coconut to the mixture and blend briefly to incorporate it.

Pour the mixture into silicone molds or ice cube trays.

Sprinkle a small amount of shredded unsweetened coconut on top of each mold or tray for added texture and presentation.

Place the molds or trays in the freezer and let them set for at least 4 hours or until completely frozen.

Once frozen, remove the mango-coconut sorbet from the molds or trays and transfer them to an airtight container or freezer bag for storage.

Serve the gourmet mango-coconut sorbet to your dog as a luxurious and refreshing treat.

Pumpkin and Coconut Milk Ice Cream

Get ready for a taste of fall in frozen form. This pumpkin-coconut delight is like a spiced latte for your pup—minus the caffeine, plus all the tail-wagging joy. One scoop, and they'll be howling for more "pupkin latte" magic.

Ingredients

1 cup pumpkin puree (see The Basics chapter for recipe)

3/4 cup unsweetened coconut milk

1/2 teaspoon ground cinnamon

Directions

In a bowl, combine the pumpkin puree, coconut milk, and ground cinnamon.

Stir the mixture until well blended.

Pour the mixture into individual serving bowls or silicone molds.

Place the bowls or molds in the freezer for at least 2-3 hours, or until the ice cream is firm.

Serve this cool pumpkin-coconut delight to your pup, and watch them savor every bite—it's their very own 'pupkin latte' moment of bliss.

Very Berry Pupsicles

These pupsicles are the ultimate fruity cool-down for your pup. Bursting with berry flavor in every lick, they're the perfect treat for hot days and happy tails. Just beware: one taste, and your dog might expect a daily "pupsicle hour."

Ingredients

1 cup mixed berries (such as blueberries, strawberries, raspberries)

1 ripe banana

1/2 cup plain yogurt (make sure it does not contain any artificial sweeteners like xylitol, as it can be toxic to dogs)

1 tablespoon honey (optional, for added sweetness)

Directions

Wash the berries thoroughly to remove any dirt or pesticides. If using strawberries, remove the stems and cut them into smaller pieces.

Peel the banana and slice it into chunks.

In a blender or food processor, combine the berries, banana, plain yogurt, and honey (if using).

Blend the ingredients until you have a smooth mixture. If the mixture is too thick, you can add a splash of water to thin it out.

Pour the mixture into ice cube trays, silicone molds or into individual serving bowls suitable for your dog's size.

Place the mixture in the freezer and let it set for at least 2-3 hours or until completely frozen.

Serve the berry pupsicle to your pup for a refreshing, fruity treat—perfect for keeping cool and staying happy on any day of the week.

Cooling Tips for Hot Days

When summer temperatures soar, frozen treats can help keep your pup cool. Always supervise your dog while they're eating pupsicles to ensure they don't try to swallow big pieces. And don't forget—hydration is key, so keep that water bowl full.

Peanut Butter Banana Swirl Pupsicles

Brace yourself for the treat that'll make your pup think they've hit the snack jackpot. With a swirl of peanut butter and banana goodness, these pupsicles are so delicious, your dog might just start "innocently" sitting by the freezer... all day.

Ingredients

2 ripe bananas

1/4 cup natural peanut butter (unsalted and unsweetened)

1 cup plain Greek yogurt (unsweetened)

1 tablespoon honey (optional, for added sweetness)

Pupsicle stick ideas: dog biscuits, bully bones, carrots, beef jerky chews

Directions

In a blender or food processor, blend one ripe banana, natural peanut butter, plain Greek yogurt, and honey (if using) until smooth and well combined.

Slice the remaining ripe banana into thin rounds.

Pour a small amount of the peanut butter and yogurt mixture into popsicle molds or small cups, filling them about one-third full.

Add a layer of sliced bananas to the molds, pressing them gently into the mixture.

Fill the rest of the molds with the remaining peanut butter and yogurt mixture, leaving a small space at the top.

Insert dog biscuits, bully bones, carrots or beef jerky chews into each mold or cup, ensuring they are well positioned. If using carrots, wash and peel them first. Then, cut the carrots into strips measuring 3 inches in length and 1/2-inch in width.

Place the molds or cups in the freezer and let them set for at least 4 hours or until completely frozen.

Once frozen, remove the pupsicles from the molds or cups and serve them to your pup for a cool, creamy treat they'll savor—it's pure bliss in every lick.

Pupsicle Stick Ideas

Get creative with your pupsicle sticks! Use dog biscuits, small bully bones, carrots, or beef jerky chews. Not only are they safe for your pup, but they also add an extra layer of fun and flavor to their frozen treat.

INDEX

Acknowledgments

First, I want to express my deepest thanks to my husband, Stacy, for his love, unwavering support, and belief in this project. I also extend my gratitude to my family and friends for their encouragement and invaluable advice throughout this journey.

Special thanks to Dr. Debbie Patterson, DVM, MS—a wonderful veterinarian whose insights and guidance helped ensure the recipes in this book are as healthy and beneficial as possible for our furry friends.

A heartfelt thank you to my dear friend, Jen Okada, for her incredible dedication and creativity in designing this book. Jen, your significant time and effort have brought my vision to life in ways I couldn't have imagined. I'm so grateful for your talent, patience, and the bond of our long-time friendship, which made this collaboration even more special.

A sincere thank you to Erin Harnum for her meticulous copy editing, ensuring clarity and precision throughout these pages. Erin, your keen eye and thoughtful edits have truly elevated this book, and I'm deeply grateful for your expertise and care.

And finally, to Lewie—for teaching me the depths of love for people, the earth, and animals, and for being the heart behind this book. You will be forever missed, but your spirit will always inspire me.

ffb3a497-0297-4295-b293-a50fc4da334bR02